BRAIN GAMES®

OPTICAL ILLUSIONS

LOWER YOUR BRAIN AGE IN MINUTES A DAY

Publications International, Ltd.

IS SEEING BELIEVING?

For all of the complex and captivating things scientists have discovered, the human brain is still the most mysterious part of our bodies. One thing we do know is that the brain's interpretation of the world isn't always literal. When it comes to perception, our brain is good at filling in the gaps and drawing visual conclusions that may not match reality.

Living in our 3-dimensional world, we are constantly bombarded by common everyday optical illusions. In an effort to keep our surroundings familiar and understandable, the brain takes a few liberties here and there. And for the most part, we never notice what we are missing. In short, we oftentimes see what we want to see.

It's no wonder that optical illusions are so fascinating! They have, after all, been around for centuries and used for a number of purposes: psychological exams, creative advertisements, and just plain fun! Over the years, scientist have studied and employed optical illusions to gain insights into how our brain interprets information and builds a representation of our surroundings.

Illusions can also be utilized as educational and improvement tools. In order to decipher a typical illusion, your brain must function in ways it isn't accustomed to. Stepping outside your comfort zone and thinking in ways that are creative and challenging to your visual perception is precisely the kind of exercise needed to increase your brain's flexibility. Just as going to the gym keeps you physically fit, completing visual puzzles—here in the form of optical illusions—will keep you mentally fit. Consider it a trip to the cerebral gym!

So don't be mistaken about the illusions found in this book—they do much more than play with how we see the world. They are designed to get your cognitive motors in gear, your perception heightened, and your concentration razor sharp. And, most importantly, they're a lot of fun!

When all is said and done, you may not believe your eyes!

APPLE OF MY FACE

Do you notice anything strange about this apple core? If you look closely, you can see the profiles of 2 faces.

OFF THE WALL

As you move your eyes around this image, do these wallflowers seem to spin?

CAMOUFLAGE ILLUSION

Optical illusions occur in nature. Animals use camouflage to hide in plain sight. Can you spot a young copperhead snake in this camouflage illusion?

REVERSIBLE CHIMNEYS

You probably see two chimney tops in this image—one in the upper part and another in the lower part. Each apparent chimney leads downward. In this equivocal illusion, the image has more than one single interpretation.

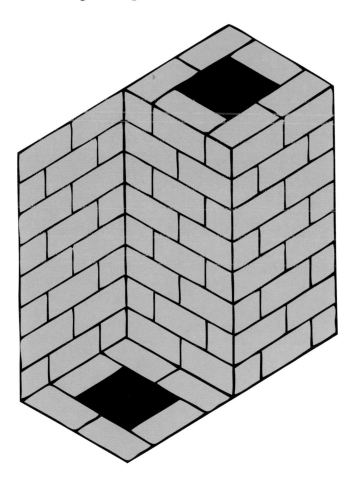

MISDIRECTION

Do these arrows appear to move in the direction in which they are pointing? That's because most of the arrows have white edges on one side and black edges on the other. These edges are responsible for the illusion of movement and the direction of the apparent movement.

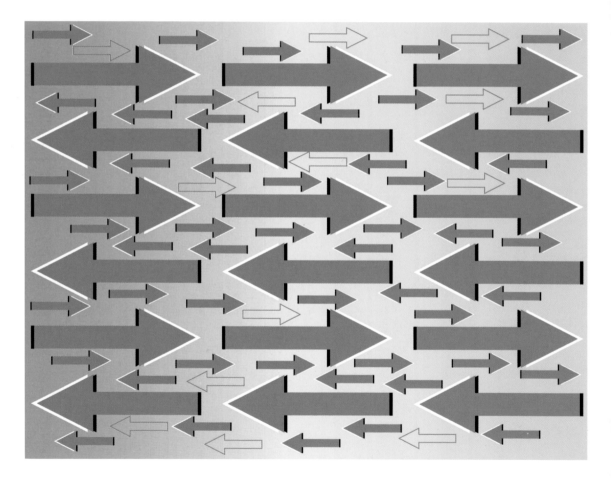

LINE LENGTHS

Which line is longer—the horizontal line or the vertical line? Though it may be hard to believe, the horizontal and vertical lines are equal length. The diamonds placed at the ends of the vertical line make it appear longer. The 3 diamonds laying over the horizontal line break this line. The interruption makes the combined parts seem shorter.

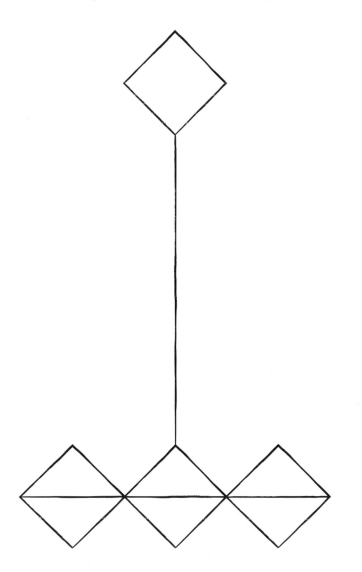

SNAKE PIPES

Don't be fooled by this illusion. These snake pipes may appear to be moving, but they are really stuck on the page.

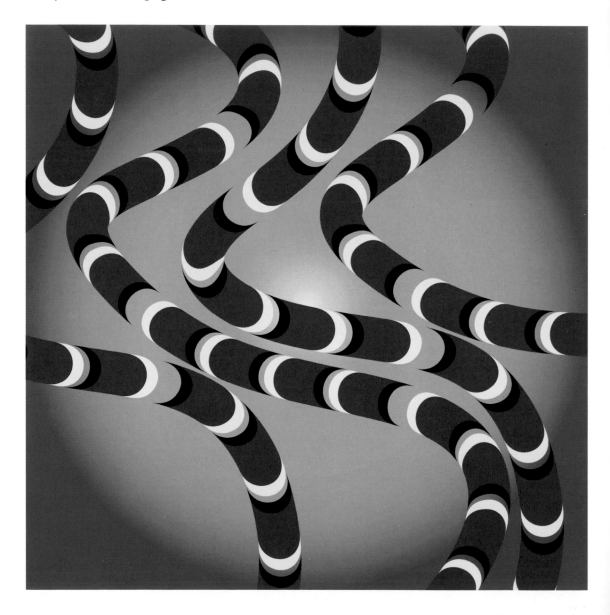

IMPOSSIBLE KNOTS

At first glance, this drawing may appear normal, but closer inspection reveals that this 2-dimensional object cannot exist in our 3-dimensional world. Impossible objects can only exist on paper.

A PUZZLING PERSPECTIVE

Which of the 3 men depicted in this drawing is the tallest?

Answer on page 160.

THE HOLE THING

The curved lines and dark center in this illusion give the impression of depth where there is none. These seemingly moving folds are static on the page.

SEAMLESS FACES

Which do you see first—the profiles of black faces or white faces? These seamless columns of faces in silhouette work upside down too.

RIDING THE WAVES

Ride the waves as these opposing curved lines give the impression of peaks and valleys. Which are the peaks and which are the valleys? It all depends on your perspective!

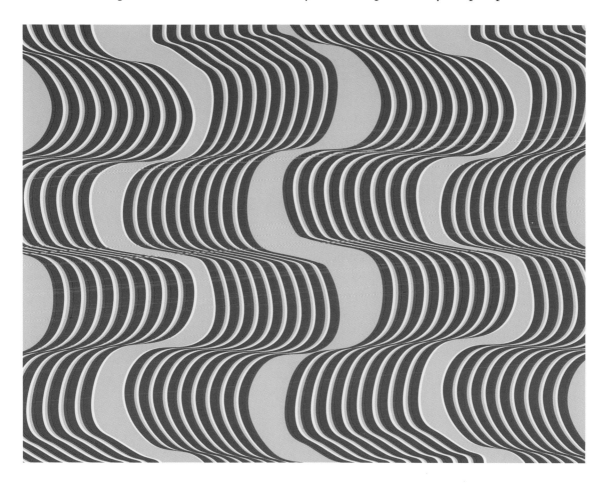

WINEGLASSES

This illusion involves how we perceive color. Our mind may lead us to believe that this distortion of color is a natural reflection, when this isn't the case.

HEART AND SOUL

The pink hearts in the top right and bottom left squares are darker than the other 2 hearts, right? Wrong! All 4 hearts are identical in color. The lighter background color in the top right and bottom left squares make the pink hearts seem darker by contrast.

FANCY FEET

Look closely. Do you notice something odd about these seemingly rotating flower petals? They are footprints—or rollerblades—depending how you look at it!

YOUNG OR OLD?

Are the old, ugly woman on the left and the beautiful, young princess on the right one and the same? Turn this page upside down to find out.

PROTRUDING PATTERN

If you let your eyes roam around, this pattern may appear to protrude out in some places and dip down in others.

LEAFY SEADRAGON

This leafy seadragon blends right in with its marine habitat. Its long, leaf-like protrusions serve as camouflage.

SNEAKY SNAKE

The snake inside this square appears to have shape. But this is only a manipulation of space and dimension! By readjusting some lines, it appears that a snake has risen out of the background.

A WHIRLING WORLD

Shift your eyes around this image. Do you notice that different elements begin to move?

CRISS-CROSS

Though the middle gray boxes appear to be different shades of gray, it's just an illusion—they are all the same shade.

BALLOONACY

As you fix your gaze on different areas of this image, you may notice how the balloons seem to sway back and forth.

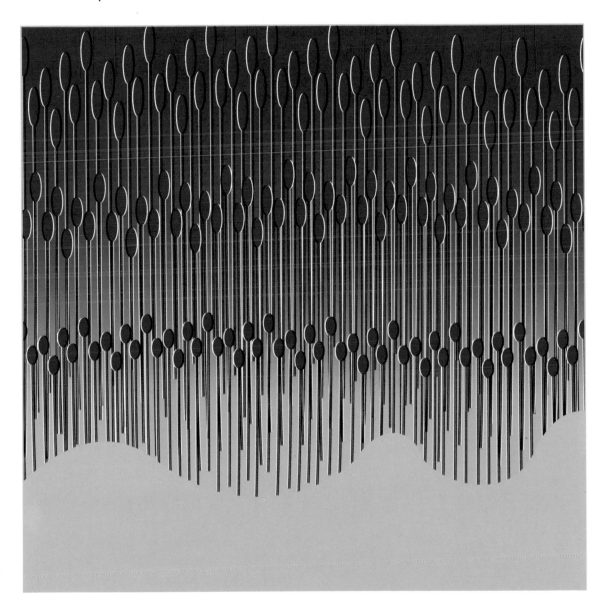

IMPOSSIBLE FIGURE

This figure is easy to draw, but impossible to make. That's because it's an impossible figure that can only appear in 2 dimensions.

CHESS PIECES

There is something ambiguous about this image. What do you see—a partial set of chess pieces or 2 people leaning in for a chat? It could be either. The appearances of many illusions are largely shaped by perception.

SEEING STARS

Gazing at this swirling motif too long will have you seeing stars!

CONVERGENT ALIGNMENTS

Do the 2 alignments of black and white segments move toward one another at the top? Or are they parallel?

Answer on page 160.

SOMETHING SWELL

Take a good look at this image—do parts of this wheel seem to swell and extend outward?

A SHADY SHAPE

Our brains use clues like shading to turn 2-D images like this into something that looks 3-D. Based on our past experiences with shading, our brains can jump to the incorrect assumption that this shape has depth.

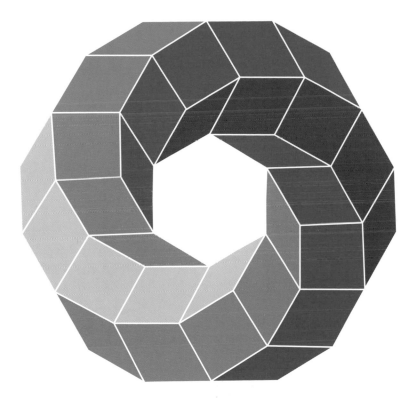

GET TO THE POINT

Though this shape appears to be coming off the page, it's just an illusion. Thanks to perspective and space manipulation, the focal point appears to be on the rise, or in retreat, depending on how you look at it.

ROLLERS

Stare at these dots and you'll probably see 3 vertical columns that roll back and forth.

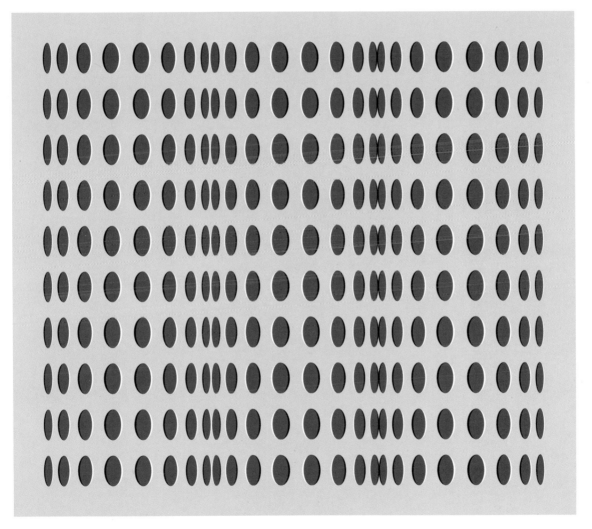

HANDS IN PRISON

You may not spot anything wrong with this image at first glance. But upon further inspection, you'll notice something problematic. The black hands and black bars can't exist simultaneously with the white hands and bars.

SPRINGTIME SPINNERS

Shift your eyes around different parts of this image. Do these flowers seem to spin around when viewed with your peripheral vision? The combination of light and dark edges underneath the bright petals created this apparent movement.

IMPOSSIBLE SHELF

We all know that sometimes pictures lie. This clever optical illusion is one such example. Nothing about this shelf appears unusual at first, but a closer look at the lower right corner proves this shelf is impossible.

TWIN GIRAFFES

At first glance, this appears to be 2 conjoined giraffes sharing a common pair of legs. Upon further inspection, we can see that the front legs of the closest giraffe are blocking the front legs of the giraffe behind it.

DECEPTIVE DOTS

If you let your eyes roam around this image, you're likely to experience a warping effect. This is known as anomalous motion, a term used to define the appearance of motion in a static image. Color contrasts and eye movement contribute to relative motion effects.

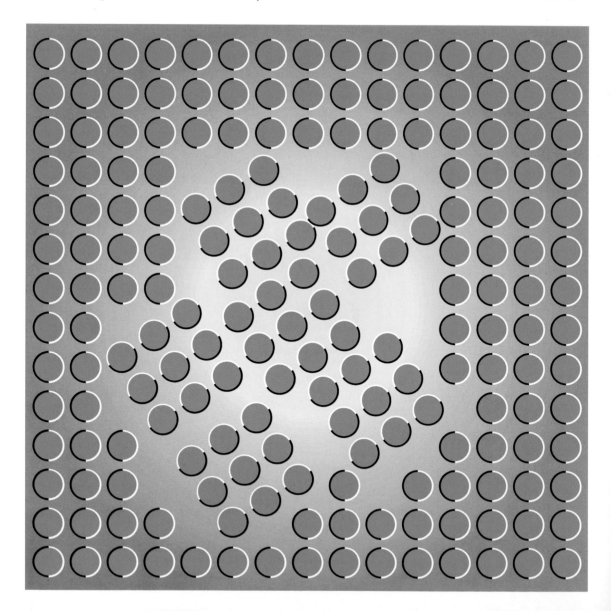

LOOK CLOSELY

Look closely—can you identify the 2 animals hidden within this optical illusion?

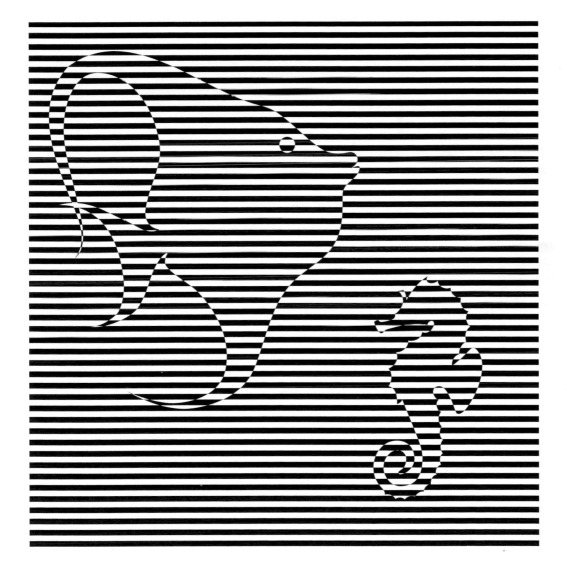

Answer on page 160.

ZIGZAG BALLS

This illusion takes advantage of the way your brain converts 2-D images from your eyes into 3-D images. You see these balls as 3-D spheres rather than 2-D circles because your brain makes assumptions based on what these objects look like in real life.

UPSIDE DOWN WORLD

Refraction is a mind-blowing idea. In this illusion, spherical refraction occurs because light passes through this glass sphere and flips the image upside down.

FOUR SQUARE

Do the focal points of each inner square seem to protrude outward? Don't be fooled by this illusion—some carefully placed lines are responsible for this effect.

RADIAL MOTION

You may get the impression of radial motion when you stare at the center of one of these circles and move your head closer and farther away.

LOOK-ALIKES

These spiral designs look like mirror images. Can you spot the difference between them?

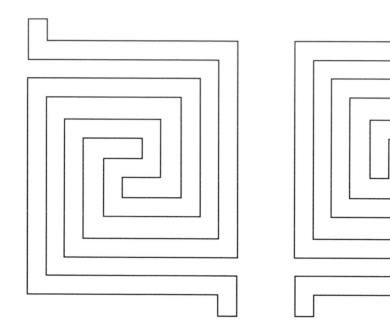

Answer on page 160.

GOING BUGGY

Staring at this illusion too long will make you go buggy! As your eyes drift around this image, do you notice the bugs in your peripheral vision moving?

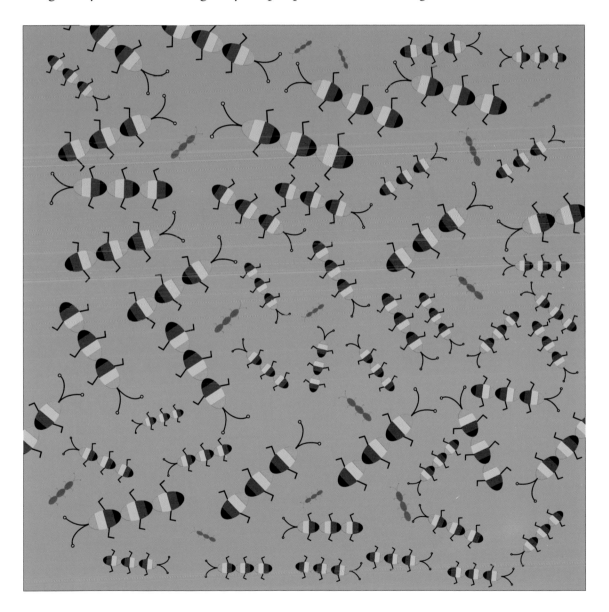

NECKER CUBE

How would you go about building a cube like this? You wouldn't get far—this is an impossible figure. The ambiguity of the Necker cube is an example of how the brain can misread visual signals.

TWO-FACED

How many women do you see? This illusion shows 2 rows of faces. Which row are your eyes drawn to first—the white profiles on the black background, or the black profiles on the white background? It's all in the eye of the beholder!

BLOOMING MAGIC

Look closely—but not too closely—at this illusion. It looks like these colors are magically bursting off the page! Move closer and farther from the image. Do you see these waves of color spin around?

SAND DUNE DISGUISE

What animal is hidden in these sand dunes?

Answer on page 160.

A STORMY ILLUSION

Let your eyes bolt around this image. Not only do the thunderbolts seem to have depth—they also seem to move!

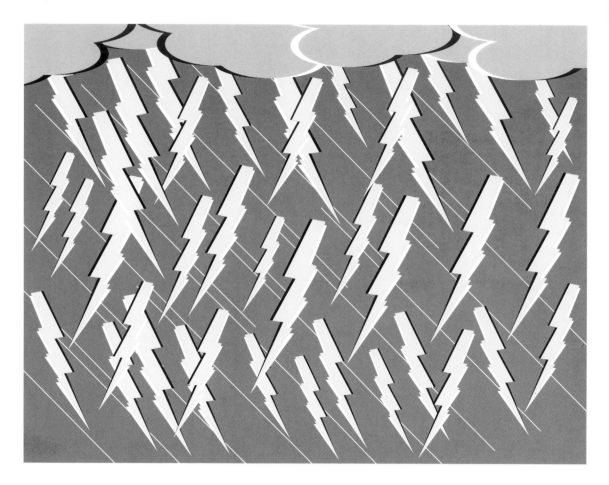

ENDLESS STAIRS

Reaching the top step in this staircase is impossible. No matter how far you climb, you will never get anywhere. This staircase is endless.

SEEING STRIPES

When lines are shifted in this 2-D figure, a pair of children's pajamas pop out of nowhere. The pajamas appear to hover above the vertical lines in the background.

GOLDEN CIRCLE

When viewed with your peripheral vision, you may notice the apparent rotation of the outer rings in one direction and the inner rings in the opposite direction. This is called a peripheral drift illusion.

SPIRAL OP ART

Optical art, or op art, makes use of lines, forms, shading, and space to produce optical effects like this seemingly swirling spiral.

GOOD VIBRATIONS

Does this vibrating illusion have you feeling queasy?

IMPOSSIBLE TRIANGLE

This triangle, no matter how you look at it, cannot exist in the real world. It may look normal at first, but no real triangle can have sides that meet in such a way.

HIDDEN AMPHIBIAN

Mother Nature helps camouflage this creature. Can you find an amphibian hidden among these floating leaves?

SAILING ALONG

It's smooth sailing for these boats. Do you notice how these rows of sailboats seem to travel back and forth?

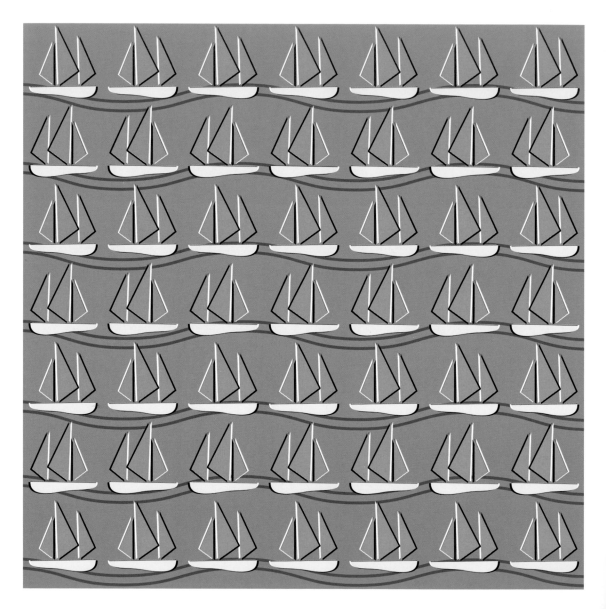

FLOATING TRIANGLE

Do you see an upside down white triangle floating above the background triangle? That's because these separate fragments evoke the perception of edges where there are none. Our brains fill in the gaps and create a triangle that isn't there.

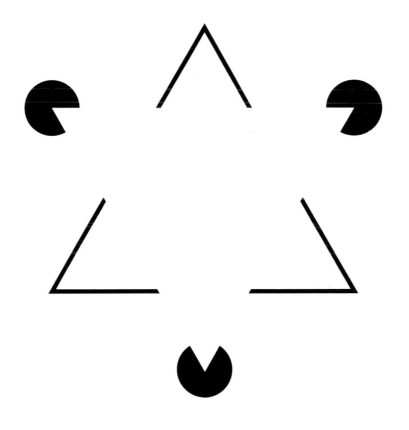

SPINATHON

Get your bearings straight as you take a spin through these seemingly moving circles.

STAIRCASE TO NOWHERE

These stairs don't go anywhere—except to the same level.

PUZZLE PIECES

Are these 2 puzzle pieces the same color?

Answer on page 160.

UPSTAIRS DOWNSTAIRS

These jagged lines and alternating colors look like stairs. But the varied length of the lines and warped perspective make them impossible.

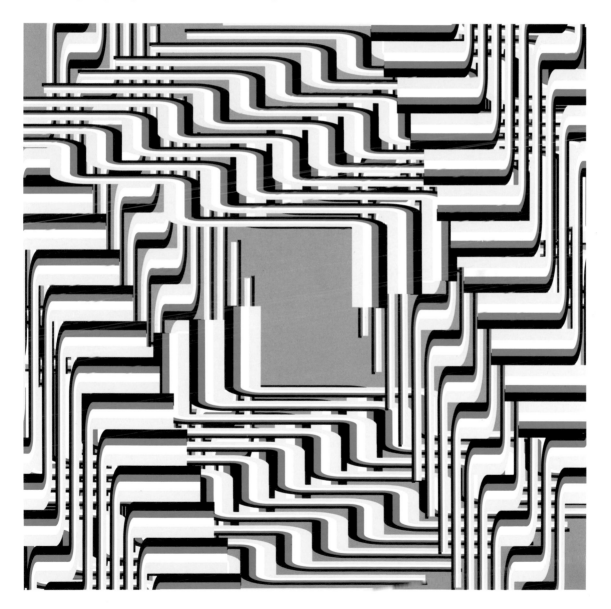

CUBE HOUSES

Are these cube-shaped houses tilted forward or backward? Either way, the angle of this photograph makes it look like these houses must have slanted floors.

FLASHING DOTS

Stare at this grid long enough and the dots will flash on and off. This is an afterimage illusion and a contrast illusion. The white dots look brighter because they are surrounded by a lot of black. This enhances the afterimage illusion.

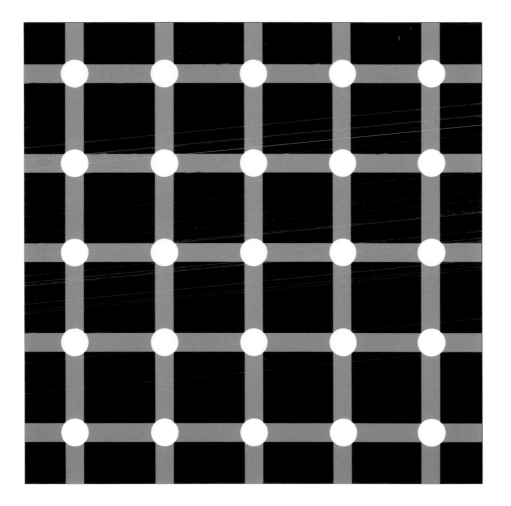

TREE MOTH

Can you find the camouflaged moth on this tree?

THE PULSE

It only takes a glance to notice something unusual with this picture—namely that the diamond shapes appear to be pulsing.

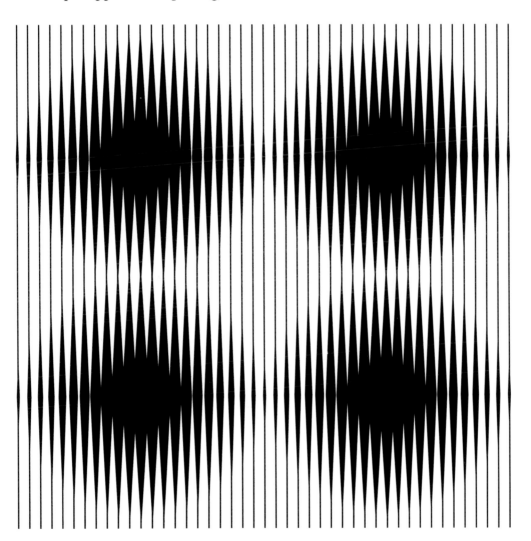

SPINNING ZIGZAGS

Sweep your eyes around this image. Do you notice how the brightly colored zigzag wheels seem to spin?

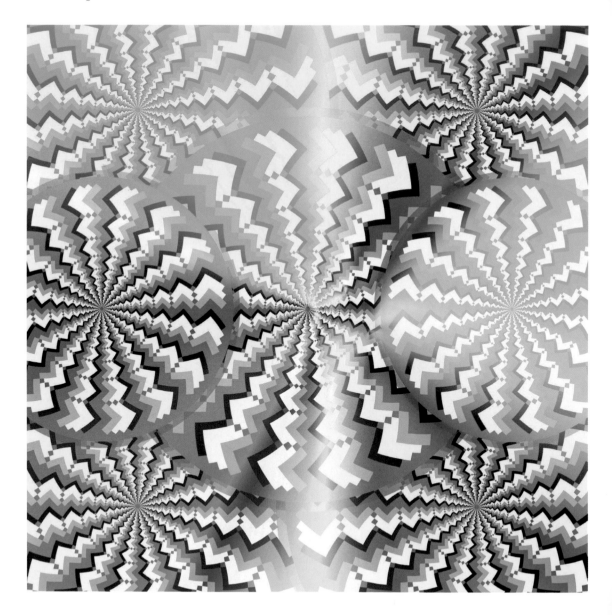

DEPTH PERCEPTION

This 2-dimensional image appears to have 3-dimensional depth. The spiral column in the center looks as if it could leap off the page.

MOVING MUSHROOMS

Though static on the page, these rows of mushrooms seem to move from side to side.

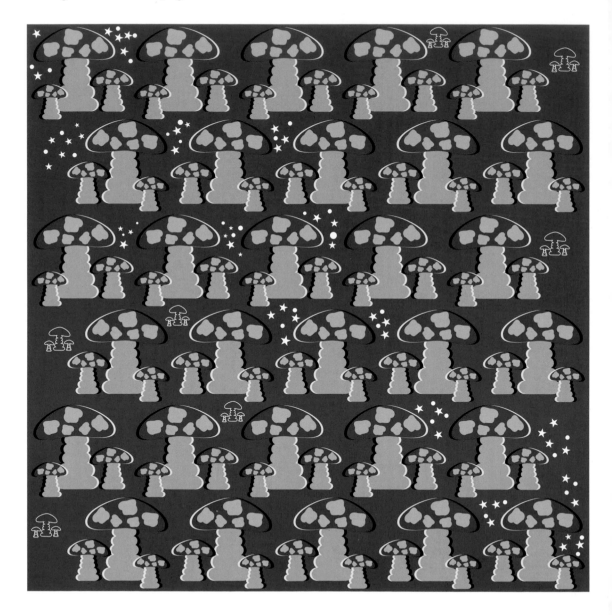

FLOATING CASTLE

This castle looks like something out of a fairy tale. Is this a tiny castle or an enormous fountain? The fountain is much closer to the camera than the castle, creating the illusion that the castle is resting on the fountain.

IMPOSSIBLE PERCH

What's wrong with this drawing?

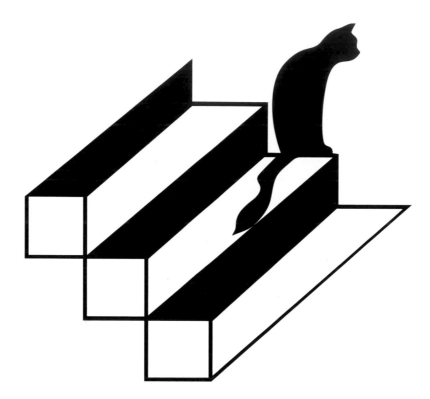

Answer on page 160.

A DIZZYING SIGHT

Staring at these lenses too long can make you dizzy. Are your eyes spinning yet?

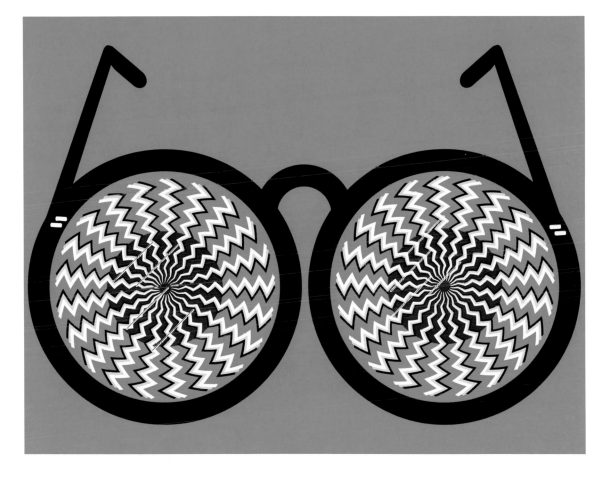

OUCHI ILLUSION

This variation on the Ouchi illusion demonstrates a brilliant contrast effect. As you stare at the image, the circle in the foreground will separate from the background and shimmer.

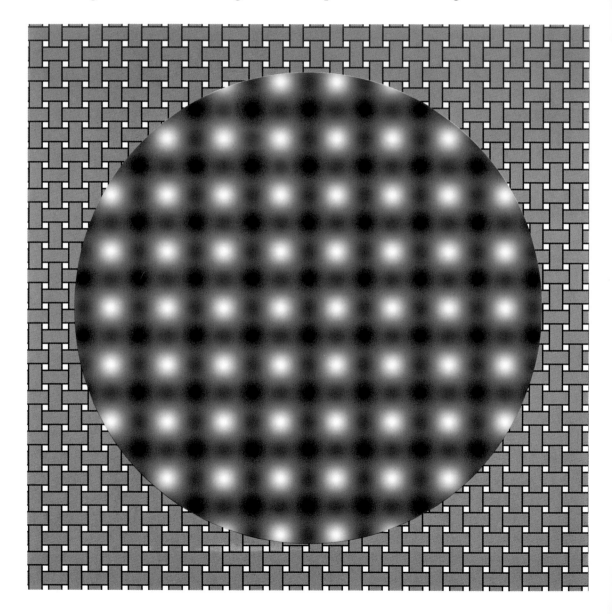

WORK SHIFT

Do these rows of workers seem to shift around? The black and white edges of the orange figures contribute to this apparent lateral movement.

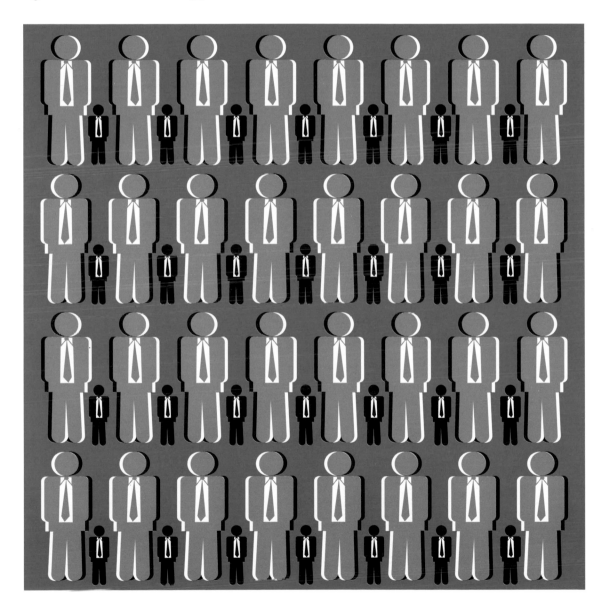

DOUBLE T

This figure defies the rules of space. Do your eyes switch between 2 perspectives—the right side up T and the upside down T? That's because this is an impossible figure.

SWIRLING BUTTERFLIES

These static butterflies seem to swirl counterclockwise on the page. Although these butterflies seem to form a spiral, they are just aligned in a series of 5 concentric circles.

INVISIBLE MAN

There's no explaining this one. This altered image leaves no trace of a man but his shadow and his shoes.

RADIAL SPIN

The alignment and shading of the different colored segments interact to create a seemingly radial motion. The bands appear to pulsate outward as they spin.

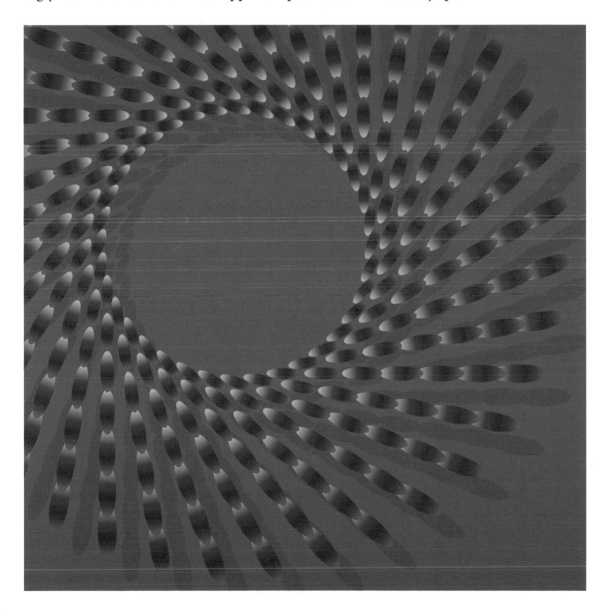

WHAT DO YOU SEE?

What do you see here? A black rectangle and 3 black squares, or something more?

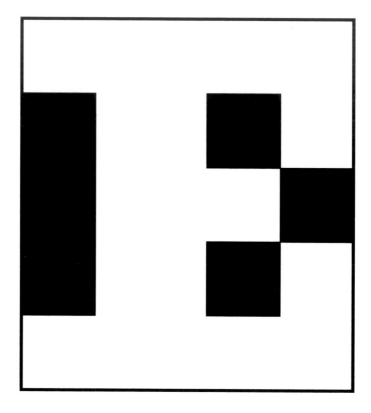

Answer on page 160.

THAT'S IMPOSSIBLE!

This impossible structure cannot exist in the 3-dimensional world. Look at how the joints meet—no real figure can have sides that meet in such a way.

MUSIC'S IN THE AIR

The wavy horizontal lines behind the notes add to the illusion of movement.

INTERRUPTED LINES

Which of the lines above is extended below?

A B C D E

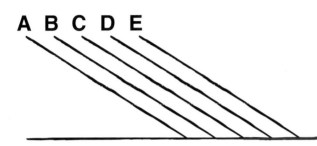

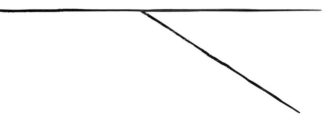

Answer on page 160.

SHIFTY EYES

As you move your eyes around this image, do the rows and columns of eyes appear to shift from side to side?

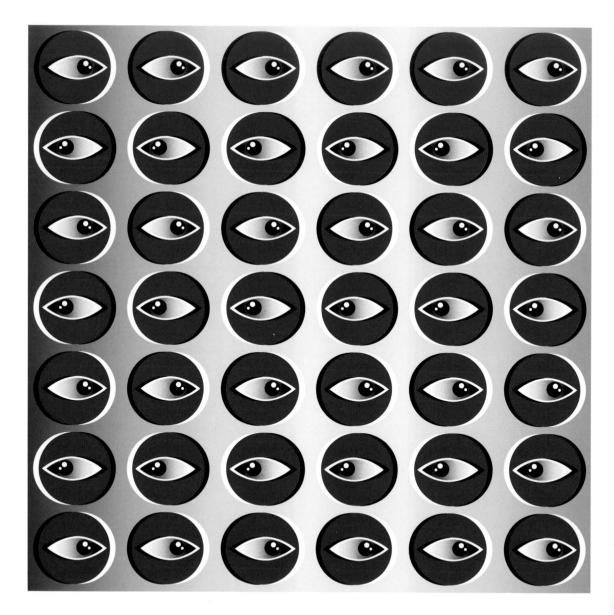

CORAL REEF CAMO

Camouflage allows this octopus to hide on this coral reef.

TO A POINT

No, this shape isn't coming off the page, it just appears to be. Thanks to some clever manipulation, the center appears to point up or down, depending on how you view it.

FACE TO VASE

This is a variation of the classic Rubin's vase illusion, named for Danish psychologist Edgar Rubin. The image can be perceived as a vase or as the profiles of 2 human faces.

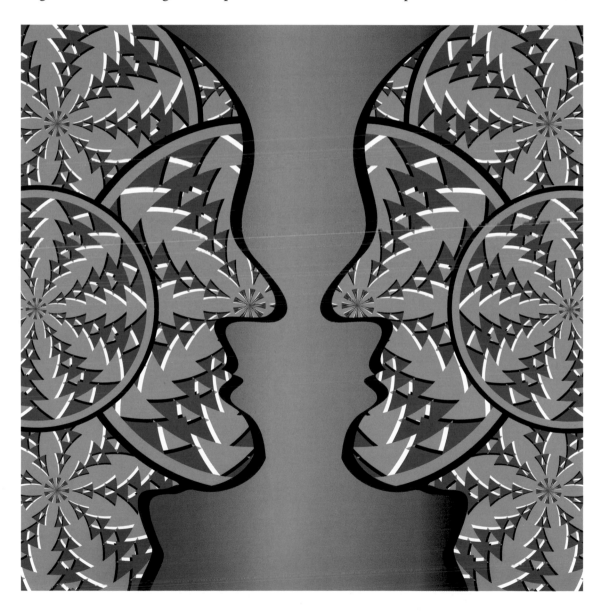

BLOSSOMING TREE

Try to keep your perspective while gazing at these swirling blossoms.

LEAF-SHAPED MOTH

This leaf-shaped Lappet moth is well camouflaged in its environment. Can you spot it?

BUSY BEE

Your brain and visual cortex are designed to detect motion even where there is none. So don't be alarmed if this cartoon bee's wings seem to flap!

ROTATING TILES

Keep your eyes moving to see the rotating effect of this design. Do you notice that the tiles have black and white edges? These edges are powering the effect. The direction of apparent movement is based on which side is white or black.

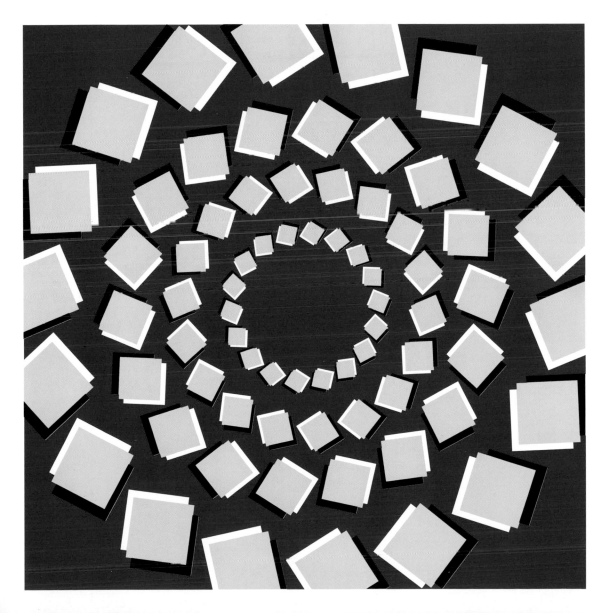

PINSTRIPES

Which is darker—the blue color in the inner square or the blue color in the outer square?

Answer on page 160.

FLUTTERING HEART

Don't let your heart flutter at the sight of these rotating hearts.

NO ESCAPE STAIRCASE

Good luck escaping from these impossible staircases!

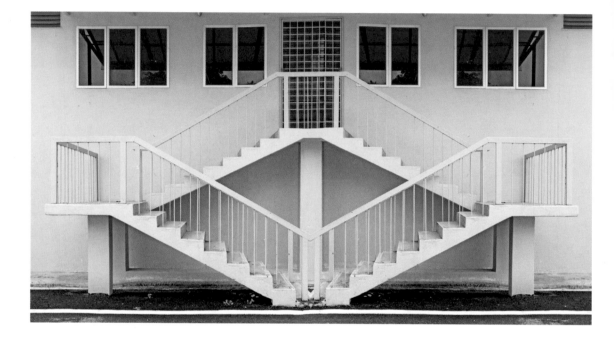

TWO VIEWS

Like many illusions, there is more than one way to view this ambiguous image. Do you see the profile of Nefertiti?

FLOATING CLOUD

Let your eyes travel around this image. Do the squares in the background appear to change?

CUBE DOTS

Do you see a cube hovering above the 8 dots? The hovering cube, which doesn't exist, is only suggested by the pattern on the black dots. Our brains automatically complete the cube from its individual elements.

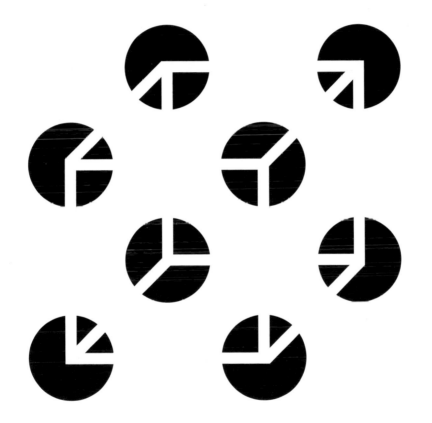

SUPERMARKET MANIA

Do these rows of shopping carts appear to move in opposite directions? The first and third rows appear to roll to the right, while the second and fourth rows seem to roll left.

IMPOSSIBLE STAR

Is this star drawn correctly? At first glance, there's nothing wrong with this drawing. But a closer look reveals that this star could never exist in the real world, except on paper.

SIAMESE ZEBRAS

This is an ambiguous illusion. Which zebra does this head belong to?

AUTUMN LEAVES

The seasons turn and so do these leaves!

A SOLITARY TAP

This magic tap in Belgium runs continuously. Although it seems to be suspended in mid-air, there is a secret pipe going up the center of the water stream. The water flows around the pipe, concealing it from view.

MELTING WHEELS

These zigzag wheels do more than spin—they seem to melt on the bottom.

MOSSY FROG

Mother Nature provides the perfect camouflage for this mossy frog. Do you see it?

SHIP SHAPE

Can you spot the hidden shape within these lines?

HYPNOTIC TUBES

Focus on the tubes below as they turn and turn and turn ...

GEARS IN MOTION

The alignment of these black and white rectangles creates the illusion of wheels turning inward and outward.

SLITHERING SERPENT

Don't be fooled by this illusion—this serpent is stationary on the page. The combination of red and purple colors is responsible for the apparent swirling.

TREE LIZARD

Can you find a camouflaged lizard on this tree? Its coloring blends in with the bark.

DEVILISH DOGS

There may be the same number of dog heads and dog tails, but there's something strange about this seamless pattern of dogs. The heads and tails don't match up!

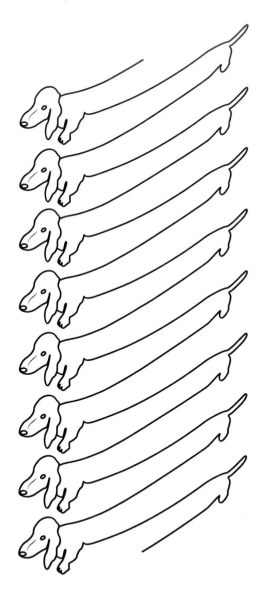

BUBBLE SWIRL

Don't fall for this trick—these swirling bubbles only give the illusion of movement.

MALIGNED CIRCLE

If you think the circle seems crimped at the points of the triangle, you are mistaken. The white circle at the center of the image is a perfect circle. It only appears to be distorted.

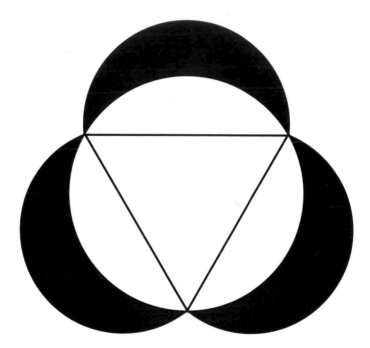

ZIGZAG WHEELS

The zigzag wheels are locked in their positions on the page, but that doesn't stop them from appearing to rotate.

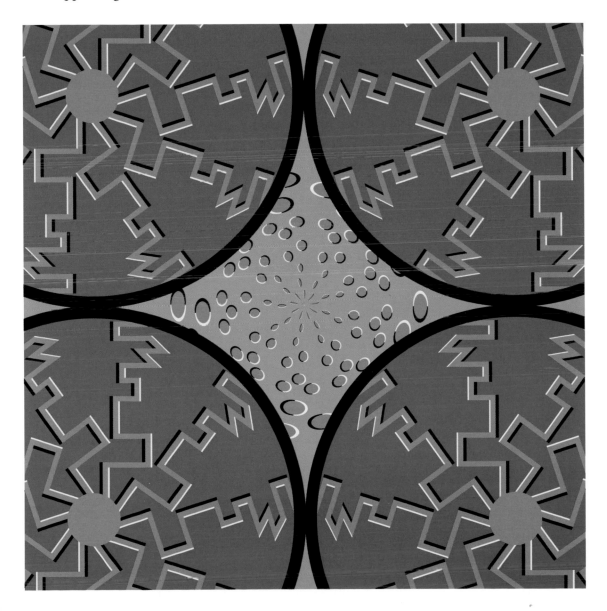

IMPOSSIBLE RING

This drawing looks convincing, but this ring is just another impossible shape.

COLUMN CONFUSION

These columns seem to bend and bow, but do they really? Nope, these columns are perfectly straight and parallel to each other. It's the slanted lines inside the columns that trick our eyes.

JUGGLER

This juggler has accomplished an impressive feat—making the balls appear to move!

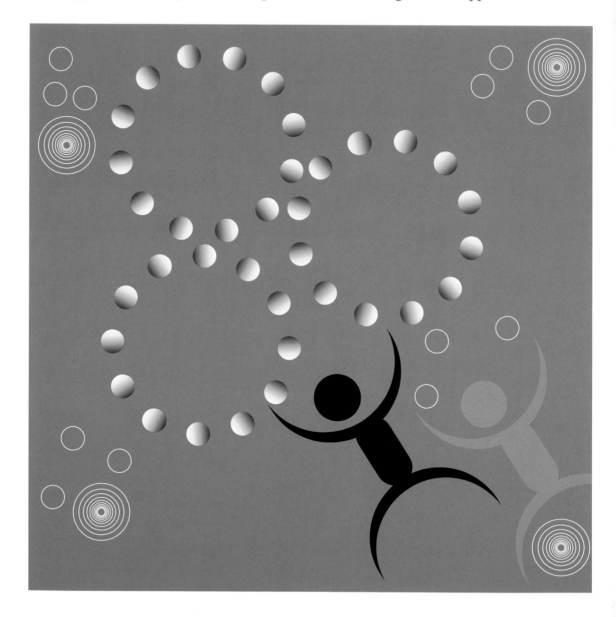

ON THE WALL

It looks like this woman is doing the impossible—sitting upside down on the wall. The key word is "impossible." This is just a creative photo.

IMPOSSIBLE TOY

You won't find this impossible design at your local toy store.

BLUE DIAMOND JUBILEE

Shift your eyes around this image without focusing on one place too long. Do you notice how the blue diamonds seem to spin?

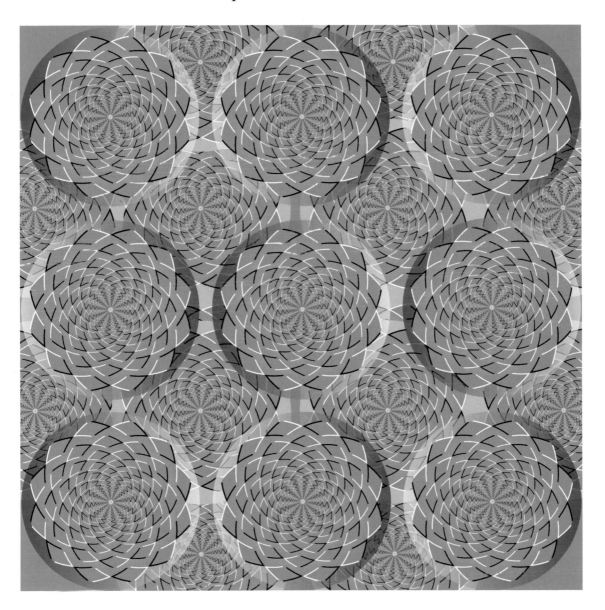

TUNNEL VISION

Do you see a tunnel in this image? This spiral design only gives the illusion of depth.

DANCING STARS

Look at these dancing stars shine. Do you see how the rings of stars appear to rotate? Try moving closer and farther from the image. You may notice the rings will counter-rotate.

IMPOSSIBLE FOUNTAIN

This is another impossible structure, here in the form of a flowing fountain. There's no way the rear columns could be on a separate plane than the front columns.

HOLE IN ONE

This illusion is the result of some creative photography.

TRAFFIC JAM

Notice how these blue cars seem to move from dark to light.

SEAMLESS PATTERN

This is a take on the impossible image. Notice how the arrangement and shading of wood cubes gives the illusion of depth.

TRIANGULAR TWIRL

Why not give this motion illusion a try?

IMPOSSIBLE CYLINDER

Here is another figure that, while looking correct at first, is actually impossible to create.

APPLE SUSPENSION

No, this apple isn't suspended in mid-air. This is another clever photo illusion.

PARTICLE THEORY

Look at this image—but not too closely—do you see these shapes moving?

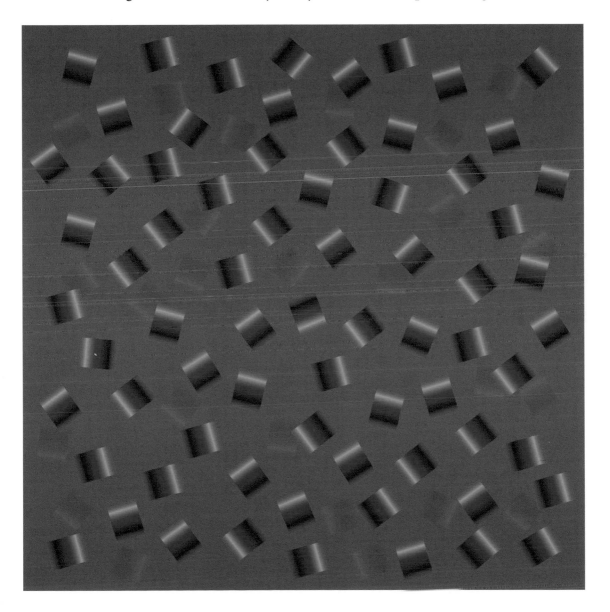

DOUBLE V

Look at the 2 Vs. Are they the same color?

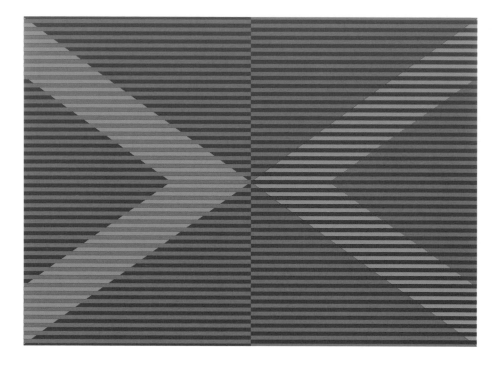

Answer on page 160.

RUNNING WATER

This zigzag pattern gives the impression of running water. Gaze at this image and watch the water flow.

INTERTWINED

What's wrong with this figure? It can't exist in 3 dimensions.

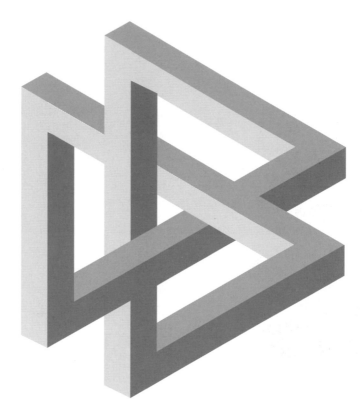

HOW MANY ARROWS?

How many arrows can you see? Are you sure? Count them again.

Answer on page 160.

ON DECK

If you want to stare into this spiral design, suit yourself.

PEACOCK PERSUASION

Do these bands of color radiate outward or inward? You decide!

A LEAFY ILLUSION

This lizard blends right in with its leafy surroundings.

HIDDEN BUTTERFLY

This butterfly was created by shifting some lines out of their vertical placement.

SUN SAIL

Notice how the blue shapes seem to move from dark to light. Can't see any movement? Try looking at the image with your peripheral vision as you move your head side to side.

JUST A FAÇADE

Look at this high-rise. Can you see the distorted reflections of the adjacent high-rise?

BOUQUET BACKGROUND

Don't be alarmed by these seemingly swirling blooms.

A DEVIOUS DISGUISE

Can you spot the devil scorpionfish hiding in this reef? Its disguise allows it to blend in with its surroundings.

WHEELS IN MOTION

Take a ride through this motif of winding wheels.

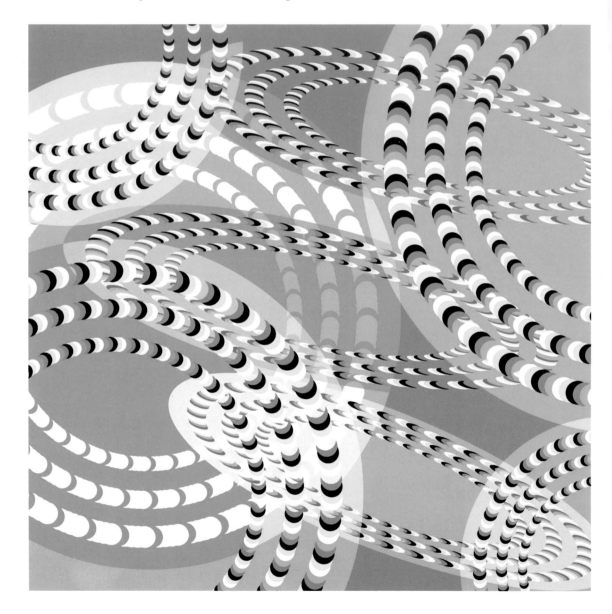

WARPED SPOON

Illusions aren't just tricks of perception and distorted effects. Sometimes, science is involved as well. The spoon below is distorted due to what's known as refraction—a property that causes light to bend. Because of the differences in density between the spoon in the water and the spoon outside the water, light bends it in different ways, causing a warped appearance.

CAFÉ TILES

These yellow and blue tiles look uneven. You can check them with a ruler; they are perfectly straight. They only appear to run at angles due to the off-center design of the yellow and blue tiles. This distortion was discovered on the tiled wall of a café in England.

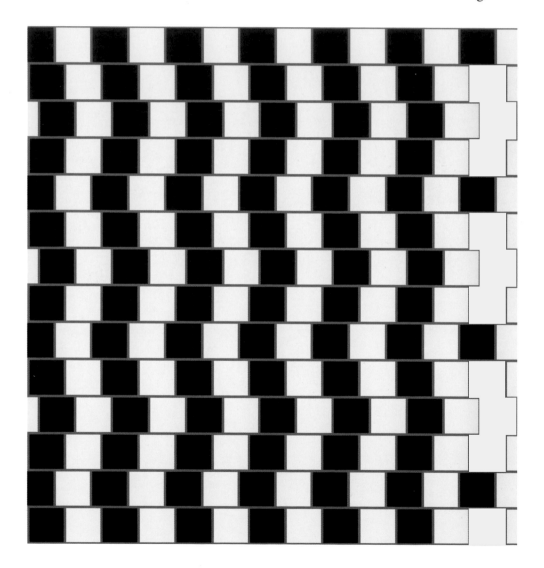

TRICKY TABLES

Do these tabletops have the same length and width?

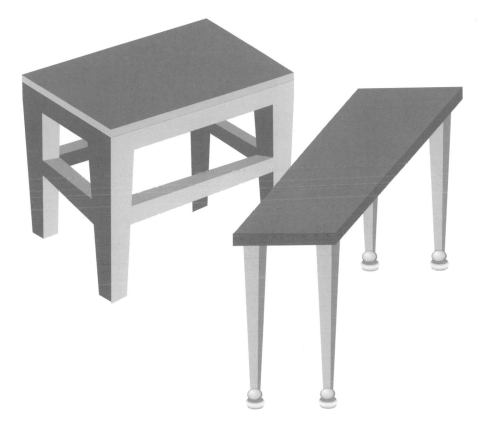

Answer on page 160.

WHICH WAY IS UP?

Are these tiles facing up or down? Also, study the top and bottom rows. The tiles aren't completely outlined. Because the middle tiles are complete, your mind fills in the gaps.

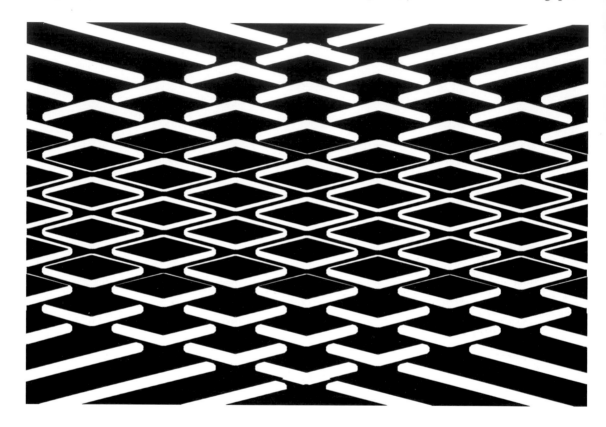

CIRCLE DANCE

Are these dancers all moving in the same direction? If you move the page closer and farther from your eyes, the dancers counter-rotate.

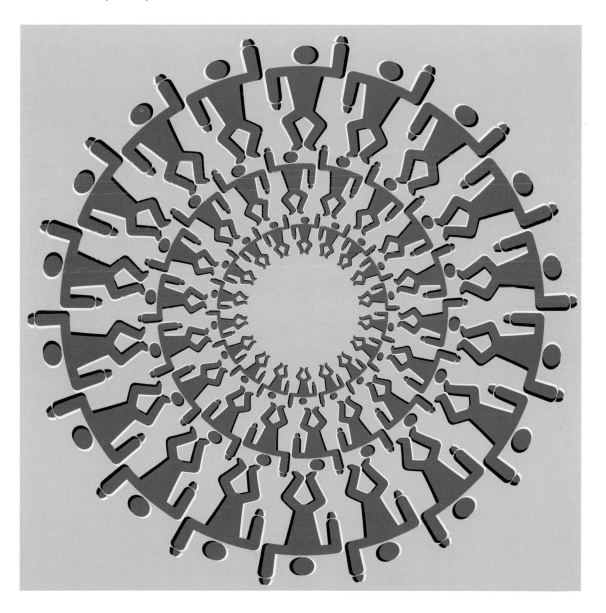

STAR AT THE END OF A TUNNEL

Does the star in this image appear to be at the end of a tunnel? That's because the successively smaller hexagons create an illusion of depth. The star is seen as being at the most distant point.

SPINSCAPE

Check out the circles below. Are your eyes spinning?

IMPOSSIBLE SHAPE

Here's another seemingly 3-D shape you'd have trouble building.

INFINITE REFLECTIONS

This illusion was achieved by this woman holding a mirror over her face in front of a larger mirror, creating the impression of infinite reflections.

COMMON CAMO

Camouflage allows this common looper moth to rest easy.

UNDER THE SEA

These little fish seem to swim back and forth without effort. The background color may have something to do with that!

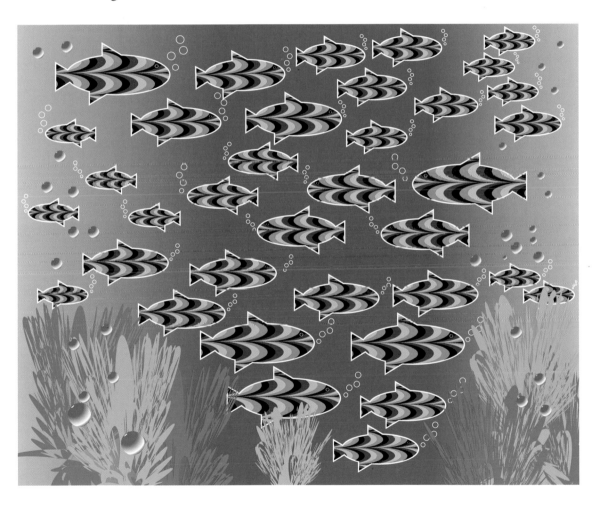

GLASSWARE

What do you see—purple wineglasses or white vases? The same contours in this figure produce purple wineglasses and white vases.

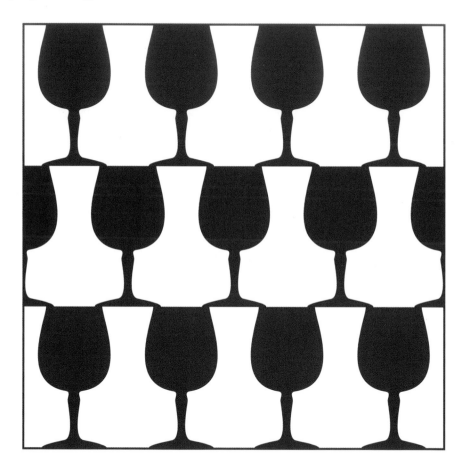

SUNBURST

This op art sun is bursting with color—and spinning too!

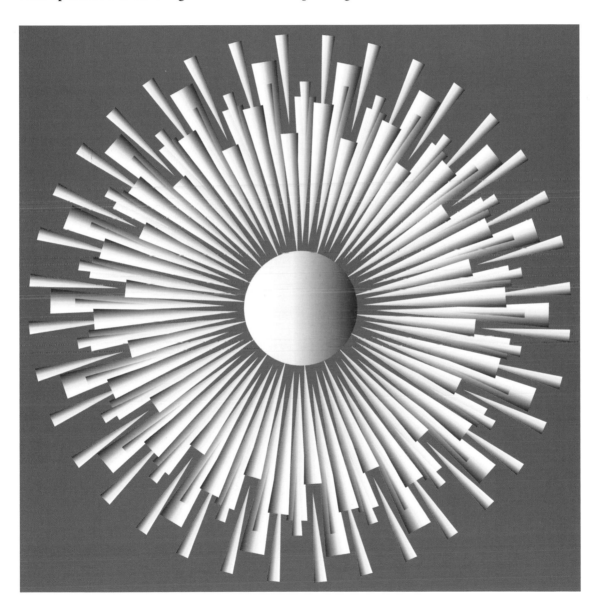

ALIEN INVADERS

These alien invaders are tough to shoot. They seem to be moving from side to side.

A PIECE OF CAKE

When you look at this ambiguous drawing, you may see a cake with a piece cut out. Turn the drawing upside down and you suddenly see a single piece of cake on a plate. In this equivocal illusion, the drawing has more than one interpretation.

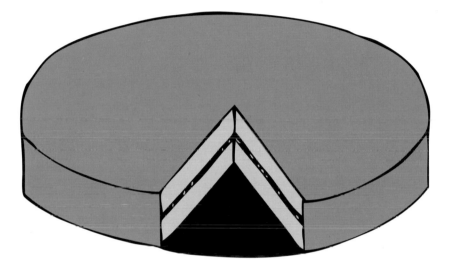

MAGENTA IN MOTION

Though static on the page, these zigzag lines seem to rotate.

WHAT ARE THE ODDS?

This is a variation of the Penrose triangle. What are the odds this triangle could exist in 3-D? Not good.

ANSWERS

A PUZZLING PERSPECTIVE (Page 12)

The 3 men are all the same size. The perspective lines drawn behind the men trick us into thinking the top man is farther away and therefore the tallest. This illusion suggests we judge size based on its background.

CONVERGENT ALIGNMENTS (Page 29)

The 2 vertical alignments of black and white segments are perfectly parallel to each other.

LOOK CLOSELY (Page 39)

Angelfish and seahorse

LOOK-ALIKES (Page 44)

The lines in the left spiral are continuous; the lines in the right spiral have 2 separate parts.

SAND DUNE DISGUISE (Page 49)

An elephant is hidden on top.

PUZZLE PIECES (Page 62)

Yes, the puzzle pieces are the same color. The light colored bars crossing the top piece and the dark colored bars crossing the bottom piece impact how we see the identical color of both puzzle pieces.

IMPOSSIBLE PERCH (Page 72)

The stairs, and the cat's perch upon them, are impossible. These stairs could not be built with raw materials.

WHAT DO YOU SEE? (Page 80)

The letter E; flip it upside down and you'll find the numeral 3.

INTERRUPTED LINES (Page 83)

Most people think that the answer is D, but A is the correct answer.

PINSTRIPES (Page 92)

The blue color is the same throughout the figure. The black stripes in the inner square and the white stripes in the outer square influence the way we perceive the blue color.

DOUBLE V (Page 130)

Yes, they are the same color. But both are influenced by the surrounding colors.

HOW MANY ARROWS? (Page 133)

8

TRICKY TABLES (Page 145)

Yes, trace them if you're not convinced!